Learn to

A NUMBER
CONSCIOUS
LIFE

Discover a deeper understanding
of yourself and your relationships
through the language of
numerology.

LILI ANN SAYERS

CONTENTS

NUMEROLOGY INTRODUCTION

On the 12th of the 12th in 2012 I remarried for the 3rd time. My friends thought that I had picked this date to make sure that my husband would always remember our anniversary, but the real reason was because in the fascinating world of numerology it is believed that this number is immensely powerful and represents completion. Some would say 3rd time lucky, but I needed all the help I could get to ensure that this time my marriage would be successful, and I am pleased to say that so far so good!

I did not realise until after our marriage that our ages were also significant! I was 48 so if you reduce 48 down by adding them together, 4+8 = 12 and my new husband was 57, so reducing his number down, 5+7 = 12! So, the number 12 was most definitely our magic number!

If you pause for a moment and think about it, we live in a world full of numbers! Numbers are all around us. From the moment that we are born we are allocated our very own numbers, through our date of birth which stays with us throughout our lives and is used to help identify ourselves to the outside world. The first thing most of us do when we wake up is to look at the time, also shown to us by a number. Our diaries and calendars are full of numbers and are an important part of planning our day, taking, and picking up our children from school, going to work, having breakfast, lunch, and dinner, meeting our friends and family, and going to sleep. Numbers affect everything that we do, right down to the numbers on our front doors identifying where we live to the numbers in our mobile phones connecting us with our friends, family, and business associates and also not forgetting the numbers that we hold in our bank accounts! Numbers have become an essential part of our everyday lives and we really could not manage without them.

Numbers and the art of numerology can totally change our outlook and can reveal so much to us about ourselves, our friends, work colleagues and our family. You do not need to be a mathematician to benefit from numerology and with just an easy calculation that I will reveal to you later, you will be able to have a better understanding of yourself and those around you, uncovering personalities, strengths, weaknesses, behaviours, and talents.

From an early age Numerology had always fascinated me, however my life was taken down a different path, when at 24 years old, I lost my 18-month-old daughter unexpectedly. My whole world fell apart overnight. All my hopes and dreams for her were shattered in an instant. I found myself struggling with my loss and emotions and just focussed on getting through the day. Two years later my son was born, and it was such a happy time, however this was short lived as I was left struggling to cope with the relentless worry of a similar outcome for him. When my son was 18 months, my marriage failed. This followed a second failed marriage some years later. Coping with the reality and responsibility of being a single parent, working full time and juggling childcare, took up the best part of my twenties and thirties. I paint a bleak picture and when I look back it was, and one that I never thought I would recover from. This was in the 80's and at that time there was no internet or social media to refer to for help or guidance and little support offered to me in the way of counselling from the medical profession. Fortunately, I was lucky that I had the love and support of my family who were always there for me and who helped me through this difficult time. I initially saw this period in my life as my wasted years, but upon reflection I now realise that it was a time of learning to understand myself, experiencing resilience, perseverance, and strength and without it sounding too cliché, has helped to make me the person that I am today.

I have spent the best part of my life trying to come to terms and to be at peace with not just the loss of my daughter and the subsequent breakdown of my marriages, but the hopes and dreams that went with it and the impact that it had on my immediate family too. I was not suffering alone. My whole family were suffering, and I carried a lot of guilt in my heart for their suffering too. My parents had lost their first grandchild, my grandparents had lost their first great grandchild, and my sister and brother-in-law had lost their only niece. It was not supposed to be like that. We all dealt with it in different ways, which at the time surprised me. However, I now understand that grief tends to rear up and show itself to others in different ways.

I believe that if I had fully understood the power of numerology, I would have understood myself and my husband and family better during this time, had stronger coping mechanisms to help me with my feelings and emotions and reacted to situations and challenges presented to me differently. It would not have taken away the pain and utter despair that I was feeling but I am sure that it would have helped me to move forward with my life sooner.

It is important to mention that you do not need to have suffered a trauma or crisis in your life to benefit from numerology, far from it! It really is like learning a new language and once you understand the meaning of your own personal numbers and the numbers of those around you, it will unlock the door to understand who you truly are. You will be able to identify your own personal strengths and weakness and understand the direction that your life is taking you. You will also be able to move forward with confidence and clarity and improve the quality of your life and those around you.

So many of us are delving deeper and looking for answers during this difficult and uncertain time in our lives and it has only been since the COVID-19 pandemic and the enforced lock down that I have had more time to reflect and to be able to research and study numerology further. Every cloud has a silver lining!

This book is a simple introduction to numerology and one that you can pick up and read within a couple of hours. If you enjoy reading this, then you may wish to investigate further, and research more in-depth theories and techniques. There are plenty of excellent books out there that can show you how using numerology in your everyday life can have such a positive impact. I have personally found it to be a revelation and I hope that you do too.

I truly hope that you will enjoy reading it as much as I have enjoyed writing it!

HOW TO LIVE A NUMBER CONSCIOUS LIFE

Numerology is a fascinating subject which can give us an insight into how we understand the meanings of numbers, and why they are so relevant to us in our lives. It works by following a simple calculation of allocating numbers to our date of birth and full birth name.

This method can be used to develop a deeper understanding of ourselves and the relationships that we have with our friends, work colleagues and loved ones. It can also help us to understand who we are as individuals and why we react to situations in a certain way, helping us to identify our strengths and weaknesses and how we deal with our relationships and our emotional needs and desires.

Understanding how numerology works can give us a big advantage in all aspects of our lives. In these uncertain times a growing number of us, are turning to numerology to understand not only more about our own personalities and compatibilities with others, but also the current situations around us and interestingly using it to determine future upcoming events in our lives. Most of us go about our daily lives without even thinking about it, however if we are faced with a crisis or our stress levels increase due to a change in our normal circumstances or routine, we can feel overwhelmed and our feelings and emotions can often spiral out of control.

Due to our individual personalities, we all react to situations differently, however by using this simple method to identify the characteristics of our numbers, it can help us to understand not only ourselves but our close family, work colleagues and friends far better by knowing who we truly are and can reveal why we think and behave in certain ways. This will enable us to cope through life's challenges and help us to work together in harmony, enriching and fulfilling our lives for the better!

WHAT IS NUMEROLOGY?

There are 3 main forms of Numerology.

The Chaldean, the Kabbalistic and the Pythagorean. We are going to focus on Pythagorean Numerology.

Pythagorean Numerology

Pythagorean Numerology is the most popular form of numerology that is used today and dates to Ancient Greece and the Pythagorean idea that everything can be expressed in numerical terms and is closely related to the invention of the Alphabet.

It is believed to have been created by Pythagoras, the Greek mathematician of the 6th century BCE. Numbers were allocated to letters in the

Greek Alphabet and later updated to the Latin Alphabet and are used in sequence, using a number formula based on calculating numbers 1,2,3,4,5,6,7,8,9,11,22 & 33.

1	2	3	4	5	6	7	8	9
A	B	C	D	E	F	G	H	I
J	K	L	M	N	O	P	Q	R
S	T	U	V	W	X	Y	Z	

This is not a complicated calculation and for someone who was not particularly good at maths at school this really is an amazingly easy process! The numbers are calculated by using your full name and date of birth. Every letter in the alphabet is allocated a number and that number is added together. (If the number is over 10 then they are simply added together until you have one number, so for example if your numbers added up to 14 you would add 1+4 = 5). However, the number 11 ,22 & 33, also known as the master numbers are not reduced.

The master numbers are understood to be extra special and are heightened and more powerful versions of the numbers 1+1 = **2,** 2+2 = **4** and 3+3 = **6** offering more potential.

Each number represents different characteristics and expressions and is used to develop a deeper understanding of yourself, your strengths and weaknesses, any obstacles that you need to overcome, your challenges, inner needs and your emotional reactions which can be a real revelation into a deeper understanding of the true you.

This will all become clear in the following chapters as we follow a step-by-step guide.

YOUR CORE NUMBERS

There are many numbers and calculations that you can use within numerology, but I am going to keep it simple and focus on the 6 major numbers that I believe are going to be the most meaningful to you and will relate to your Life Path, Destiny, Soul, Personality, Maturity and Birth Day.

Life Path Number

The life path number is the most significant number in your chart and is based on your date of birth. It is also known as the birth force number and describes the true you and the life that you are likely to lead. It is important that you calculate this number first as it will reveal what direction your life is taking you, together with your personality, strengths, and weaknesses.

Destiny Number

The destiny number is calculated by using the letters in your full birth name and is also known as your name or expression number. It indicates why you are here and what your mission and purpose in life is going to be.

Soul Number

The Soul Number is calculated by using the vowels in your name and is also known as your heart's desire and indicates the desires that influence your life.

Personality Number

Your Personality Number is calculated from the consonants in your full birth name and represents the side of yourself that you are willing to let others see.

Maturity Number

The maturity number is calculated by adding the life path number and the Destiny Number together. It refers to the later part of your life, from your mid-thirties onwards. It is an important number because it shows your future potential and your ultimate goal.

Birth Day Number

Your Birth Day Number is calculated by the day of the month of your birth date. This is another important number as it will reveal talents that can help you whilst on your life path and is also one of the easiest numbers to calculate.

CALCULATING YOUR CORE NUMBERS

Your Life Path Number

Your life path number is calculated by using your full date of birth.

This number is the most important as it will give you a true understanding of who you are and what kind of life you are going to lead. It can be both positive and negative depending on the different stages of your life and can show up as opportunities, lessons, and challenges. How you respond to them can change as you go through your life.

To calculate your Life Path Number, you need to add your full date of birth together, reducing until you are left with one number. (If the number is over 10 then they are added together until you have one number, so for example if your numbers added up to 14 you would add 1+4 = 5). However, the number 11, 22 and 33, also known as the master numbers are not reduced.

For example

Sues date of birth is 12/07/1965

12/07/1965 = 1+2 (day) +0+7(month) +1+9+6+5 (year)

1+2+0+7+1+9+6+5 = 31

Reduce 31 by adding 3+1 = **4**

So, Sues Life Path Number is **4**

YOUR DESTINY NUMBER

Your Destiny Number is calculated by using your full Birth Name. Even if you only used it for a short period and your name has changed by marriage or adoption or for whatever reason you should still use your full birth name. It is believed that your birth name is the blueprint that you were born into. If you do not know your birth name perhaps due to adoption, then use your adopted name but on the understanding that it may not hold such a strong interpretation. If you cannot relate to the destiny number calculated from your birth name, then calculate your number based on your current name and see if this resonates better.

Your destiny number is also known as the expression number and will show you your mission in life and what you will be most successful at.

This is therefore the number that you need to consider when choosing your career path.

To calculate your destiny number, you need to add the numbers of your full birth name together, and just how we calculated your life path number, reduce until you are left with one number. (If the number is over 10 then they are added together until you have one number, so for example if your numbers added up to 14 you would add 1+4= 5). However, the number 11, 22 and 33, also known as the master numbers are not reduced.

Under each letter of your name write down its numerological value as shown in the next table.

For example

1	2	3	4	5	6	7	8	9
A	B	C	D	E	F	G	H	I
J	K	L	M	N	O	P	Q	R
S	T	U	V	W	X	Y	Z	

Sues full name is Susan Ann Williams

S	U	S	A	N		A	N	N		W	I	L	L	I	A	M	S
1	3	1	1	5		1	5	5		5	9	3	3	9	1	4	1

Add up each name separately:

Susan = 1+3+1+1+5 = **11**

Ann = 1+5+5 = **11**

Williams = 5+9+3+3+9+1+4+1 = 35

Reduce 35 to 3+5 = **8**

You now add these 3 numbers together:

11+11+8 = 30 Reduce 30 to 3+0 = **3**

Therefore, Susan's destiny number is **3**

YOUR SOUL NUMBER

Your Soul number is calculated by adding up the vowels in your full birth name. A, E, I, O, U. Sometimes the letter Y is used if there are no other vowels in the syllable, for example Lynn. Also, when it is preceded by a vowel such as Tracey. W is also treated as a vowel when it is preceded by a vowel such as Fowler.

Your soul number is also known as your heart's desire and is your inner most private thoughts. Your soul number is what motivates you, your inner likes, and dislikes.

To calculate your soul number, you need to add up the vowels from your name:

For example:

The vowels in **S**u**s**an **A**nn **W**i**lli**a**m**s name are:

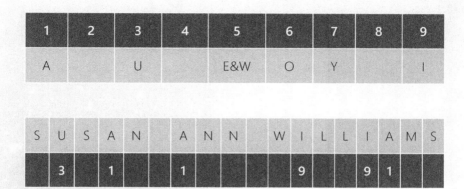

1	2	3	4	5	6	7	8	9
A		U		E&W	O	Y		I

S	U	S	A	N		A	N	N		W	I	L	L	I	A	M	S
	3		1			1				9				9	1		

Add these numbers together 3+1+1+9+9+1 = 24

Reduce 24 to 2+4 =**6**

Therefore, Susan's Soul number is **6.**

YOUR PERSONALITY NUMBER

Your personality number is calculated by using the consonants in your full birth name. Basically, these are the letters that are not vowels, however, do not include Y and W if you have used these when calculating your soul number.

Your personality number describes how you are seen by others and represents the side of you that you are willing to let others see. This means that it does not always show the true, real you, but only the side of yourself that you are willing to show so it can sometimes be difficult to identify with your personality number.

For example:

The consonants in **Susan Ann Williams** name are:

1	2	3	4	5	6	7	8	9
	B	C	D		F	G	H	
J	K	L	M	N		P	Q	R
S	T		V	W		Y		

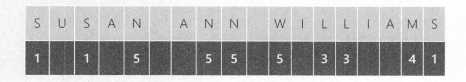

S	U	S	A	N		A	N	N		W	I	L	L	I	A	M	S
1		1		5		5	5		5		3	3				4	1

Add these numbers together
1+1+5+5+5+5+3+3+4+1 =33

33 is considered a master number and is not reduced.

Therefore, Susan's personality number is **33.**

The master number is not considered alone so when understanding the meaning of 33 you also need to understand the number that it is reduced to, so in this example it is also worth looking at 3+3=**6** too as 33 is an intensified version of 6.

YOUR MATURITY NUMBER

The maturity number is calculated by adding the life path number and the Destiny Number together. It refers to the later part of your life, from your mid-thirties onwards and is an important number because it shows you what your life is preparing you for and your future potential and ultimate goal. As you get older your maturity number will strengthen and will therefore have a greater influence on your life.

For example:

Susan's Life path number is **4**

Susan's Destiny number is **3**

Add these numbers together 4+3 = **7**

Therefore, Susan's maturity number is **7**

YOUR BIRTH DAY NUMBER

Your birth day number is a particularly important number as it signifies your own personal talents and capabilities that will help you on your life path and the type of career that you will be suited to. It is calculated by using the day of the month that you were born on.

For example:

Susan's date of birth is 12/07/1965

Reduce 12 to 1+2 = **3**

This number will have a relationship with its original double-digit number and is therefore worth exploring the numbers 1 and 2 in this example to gain a deeper insight into your numbers.

YOUR CORE NUMBERS CHART

As you start to calculate your numbers record them in the chart below. This will help you once you start to interpret the meanings later.

The Core Numbers	Your Number
Life Path Number – The birth force number. Describes the true you and the life that you are likely to lead.	
Destiny Number – Also known as your expression number, it indicates your mission and purpose in life.	
Soul Number - also known as your heart's desire and indicates the desires that influence your life.	
Personality Number - represents the side of yourself that you are willing to let others see.	
Maturity Number - refers to the later part of your life. It shows your future potential and your ultimate goal.	
Birth Day Number - will reveal talents that can help you whilst on your life path.	

THE BASE MEANINGS OF THE INDIVIDUAL NUMBERS

Now that we have calculated our individual core numbers, we can look at the meanings.

You may feel that you do not have all the qualities of your numbers or that you cannot identify with them. This is not unusual because they may not be visible to you yet. Friends or loved ones may be able to identify you within the meanings of your numbers, so ask for their opinion. Your numbers may also vary through different stages of your life and once you understand the basics of numerology there are further calculations that you can investigate that will help you to identify them, but this basic overview will give you an understanding of yourself and who you are.

The meanings of the numbers in numerology will always be the same but you will see a more in depth meaning under each core number. The easiest way to understand which meanings are most relevant to you is to look at the strengths and weaknesses under each number. You will see positives and negatives to each number, which can impact you at different stages of your life and so it is up to you to understand and to identify yourself within them.

You will also be influenced by the other core numbers in your chart and once you understand your numbers, you will be able to overcome any negative influences that may have been holding you back in your life, allowing your true numbers to be clearer to you as you move forward.

This is a simple overview of the meanings but there is so much more to numerology than this book has to offer. This is purely an introduction, and I am sure that once you understand the process you will want to delve deeper and investigate the exciting world of numerology further.

NUMBER 1 – THE LEADER

The number 1's are extremely capable, independent, creative individuals who like to stand alone and who thrive on receiving recognition. They are great visionaries who can think outside of the box although they much prefer to create and to start new projects than see things through to completion. They are achievers, full of energy, who like to be the centre of attention and who are born to lead.

Strengths:

The number 1's are ambitious and make good leaders. They are self- motivated enthusiastic, creative, strong, and independent, individuals with great potential.

Weaknesses:

They can be demanding, self-centred, impatient, and sensitive to criticism and can be opinionated with a domineering attitude.

Life Lessons to learn:

They need to learn to accept criticism and to work and lead in harmony alongside others, working on being more thoughtful, diplomatic, and considerate, controlling their domineering approach.

NUMBER 2 –
THE PLEASER

The number 2's are patient, loving and kind and love to nurture. They much prefer to feel needed and to be part of a couple as they do not like to be on their own. They are balanced and work best by co-operation and teamwork and feeling loved and appreciated by others. They can be sensitive and would rather please others and suffer in silence as they do not like confrontation.

Strengths:

The number 2's make good listeners and are caring, considerate and supportive, often mediating and becoming the peacemaker between others with their open and honest approach.

Weaknesses:

They can be jealous of others and be dissatisfied with their own achievements. They can lack common sense and be indecisive, weak, and lethargic.

Life lessons to learn:

They need to find their independence, be more assertive and be brave and say NO. Not giving too much of themselves to others and overcoming their sensitivity, will enable them to love themselves.

NUMBER 3 – THE COMMUNICATOR

Number 3's are happy, fun loving and highly sociable with excellent communication skills and are warm and friendly. They have a great sense of humour and are young at heart. They are creative and enjoy the arts and the theatre. They can light up the room with their smile and can be the life and soul of the party, however, they can tend to think of today rather than tomorrow.

Strengths:

The number 3's are popular fun loving, warm friendly sociable people. They are always optimistic and can communicate on any level to all.

▌ Weaknesses:

They can be disorganised, impatient and intolerant towards others and can be irresponsible and dramatic.

▌ Life lessons to learn:

They need to be considerate towards others, and to focus on becoming more organised and to strive for less drama in their lives.

NUMBER 4 – THE HARD WORKER

Number 4's are reliable, loyal, and conscientious hard workers who are trustworthy and will always do the honourable thing. They like everything in order and are disciplined, take their work seriously with great attention to detail and prefer to have routine and to be in control of their environment. They are dependable and make great friends who will offer you their support and understanding.

Strengths:

The number 4's are dedicated hard working reliable people who are great planners who can organise and focus on tasks enabling them to be successful.

Weaknesses:

They can be intolerant, stubborn, and inflexible and struggle to accept change through their narrow mindedness.

Life lessons to learn:

They need to show their emotions and to accept that things are not always how they would like them to be and that they need to be open minded and lighten up.

NUMBER 5 – THE FREE SPIRIT

Number 5's love their freedom and enjoy travel and meeting new people. They are adventurous and love visiting new places and learning new things. They are great communicators who can motivate people and make friends easily and are multi-talented but may struggle to stick at one thing, consequently they can suffer from a lack of direction. They are good learners and can think through complex matters and analyse them quickly.

Strengths:

The number 5's are clever and love freedom and adventure. They love to know what is going on around them and are good communicators and can motivate others.

Weaknesses:

They can get bored easily and become restless. They will take risks and struggle to stick to anything, always looking for something new.

Life Lessons to learn:

They need to learn to make plans and to prioritise, be patient, keep focused and to finish what they started.

NUMBER 6 –
THE NURTURER

Relationships and offering love and support to those around them is most important to number 6's. They are trying to bring beauty, love, and harmony into the world and are here to support the weak and the vulnerable. People who are looking for help will be drawn to them so it is important that they allocate their love and support to those who genuinely need them, or they could find themselves feeling overwhelmed and burdened.

Strengths:

You can rely on the number 6 to be kind, compassionate supportive and loving. They are always generous and responsible.

Weaknesses:

They can sometime get too involved and can interfere and become too dominant and critical, feeling resentful of their involvement.

Life lessons to learn:

They need to learn not to get too involved and to respect people's boundaries and learn to say NO.

NUMBER 7 – THE ANALYST

Number 7's are considered lucky. They are extremely analytical and require privacy and quiet time alone to research, study and to contemplate the meaning of life and the universe. They can sometimes appear aloof and detached from others however their family and home life are particularly important to them. They also enjoy spending time with nature and wildlife and are not interested in material wealth but prefer to focus more on teaching and helping others.

Strengths:

The number 7's are studious individuals who are extremely analytical and have high standards. They are intelligent, quick witted and thrive for perfection in everything that they do.

Weaknesses:

They can be reserved and anti-social, being negative and intolerant of others which can lead to them feeling lonely and isolated.

Life lessons to learn:

They need to be patient and open minded towards others, making friends and accepting other people's failures.

NUMBER 8 – THE POWERFUL

The number 8's are linked to wealth and power. They have good organisation skills and are confident working in roles with responsibility. They are successful through their boundless energy, strong determination, and hard work. They enjoy challenges and are good problem solvers and have the capability of becoming very wealthy however their rewards may not always be financial as they strive to find self-fulfilment by being self-sufficient in all aspects of their lives.

Strengths:

The number 8's are ambitious, confident, self-motivated, hardworking individuals that are extremely efficient and can be immensely powerful.

Weaknesses:

They can be greedy, ruthless, very domineering, and dictatorial with a tendency to be superficial.

Life lessons to learn:

It is important that the number 8's learn to be respectful towards others and to focus on living their lives with integrity and not being too materialistic.

NUMBER 9 –
THE HUMANITARIAN

The Number 9's have high ideals and will want to act for the greater good. They are kind, caring, loving, and generous and will always offer their help and support. They will be known to fight for the underdog and are here to give to others, unconditionally and selflessly, without receiving any reward or recognition for their efforts.

Strengths:

Nothing is too much trouble for the number 9's who are generous, sympathetic and compassionate towards others. They are not interested in material things, only seeking to offer help, and can be trusted.

Weaknesses:

They can sometimes be overly dramatic and sensitive and can become too intense and intolerant towards others.

Life lessons to learn:

They need to learn to be more tolerant of others, and to let things go and in doing so to be more accepting and forgiving.

NUMBER 11 – THE IDEALIST

This number is not considered alone and is an intensified number to the number 2 that it is reduced to, so you need to compare them together. So, 11 has all the aspects of 2 but with added charisma and inner wisdom which draws people to them. They are an intuitive idealist who expects a lot from themselves and those they are close to.

Strengths:

The number 11's are very cultured, broad minded interesting people who are charismatic creative visionaries.

Weaknesses:

They are often impractical dreamers who can be demanding with a controlling nature.

Life Lessons to learn:

They need to be more independent and assertive and learn to love themselves, not giving too much to others will allow them to find their independence.

NUMBER 22 – THE INVENTOR

This number is not considered alone and is an intensified number to the number 4 that it is reduced to, so you need to compare them together. So, 22 has all the aspects of 4 but they are also great inventors and can turn grand schemes into reality seeing them through to the end and achieving success. 22 has the potential to be the most successful of all the numbers.

Strengths:

The number 22's are inspirational visionaries who can make excellent inventors and with their great organisational skills, can help them to be focused and successful.

Weaknesses:

They can be a workaholic, with impractical expectations and can display intense, dictatorial, overbearing tendencies.

Life lessons to learn:

It is important that number 11's take the time to relax, to accept that things are not always 100% perfect and to lighten up.

NUMBER 33 – THE MASTER HEALER

This number is thought to be the most powerful number and can be exceedingly rare to find. Number 33 is not considered alone and is an intensified number to the number 6 that it is reduced to, so you need to compare them together. So, 33 has all the aspects of 6. They are master natural healers bringing love, joy, and happiness with a vision of a better world.

Strengths:

The number 33's are creative loving healers, who have great vision and a sense of purpose.

Weaknesses:

They can be self-righteous with an intolerant dictatorial, insensitive nature.

Life lessons to learn:

They need to respect people's boundaries, learn to say no and not get too involved. It is important that number 33's live with honesty and integrity.

Now that you have an understanding of the meanings of the base numbers you can now delve deeper by understanding the meanings of your core Life Path, Destiny, Soul, Personality, Maturity and Birth day numbers in the following chapters.

THE LIFE PATH NUMBER MEANINGS

Also known as the birth force number. Your life path number will describe the true you and the life that you are likely to lead.

Life Path Number 1

This is the number of an independent, strong minded, natural leader, who is extremely capable and always ready to take the lead. You are self-sufficient and like to stand alone. You enjoy being challenged and do not like to accept defeat although you may sometimes feel alone, you must learn to allow this not to affect you, instead choose to embrace your individuality.

You would make a great manager and have great entrepreneurial skills so would be good at running your own business.

Life Path Number 2

You thrive best with peace and harmony in your life. You can see both sides of a situation and make a great peacemaker as you tend to see the good in everyone. You are a good friend to have and are always willing to listen and support. It is important to you that those around you feel happy and loved. You are at your best when part of a group.

You are good at anything caring or supportive and would be a good negotiator, doctor, nurse, vet, teacher, trainer, or artist.

Life Path Number 3

Your main purpose is to bring joy and inspiration to others through your ability to entertain and your great sense of humour, creativity, and excellent communication skills. You have an inquiring nature and have many interests. You love life and are very sociable and you can make friends easily with your positive fun-loving outlook and caring nature.

You are good at anything creative, so you could be an artist, singer, songwriter, writer, actor, comedian, teacher, carpenter, or designer.

Life Path Number 4

You are a hard worker with excellent analytical and organisational skills. You take your responsibilities seriously and show great stability and discipline in your work and family life and you are full of common sense. Once you make a decision, you carry it through. You sometimes miss the bigger picture due to your focused attention to detail, but you can be at your best when dealing with a problem.

You would make a great personal assistant, accountant, architect, team leader or business owner.

Life Path Number 5

You will walk the path of freedom and exploration and will live life to the full as you are versatile and adventurous. It is important that you are free to explore and to experience everything that life has to offer and that you feel challenged and fulfilled in all that you do. You must learn not to take your freedom for granted and to be more responsible.

You can become bored and easily distracted so you will have a variety of roles to maintain your interest during your working life.

Life Path Number 6

Relationships are especially important to you and you like to take responsibility for those around you. You need to feel useful and will often sacrifice your own needs for those of others. You are always willing to help and offer your support, love and counselling and are prepared to take on much more than your fair share. You need to find a balance between helping and interfering.

You can work as a teacher, or in the care sector, such as a nurse, doctor, counsellor, midwife, or health professional.

Life Path Number 7

You are a truth seeker and love to learn and seek knowledge and information from everywhere. You can be very private and prefer your own company. You have excellent analytical skills and need time to contemplate and think things through. You can be mistrusting of others so can find it difficult to forge new friendships however you love nature and enjoy the outdoors.

You are a good problem solver and can often be found in a teaching, research, science, medicine, or an analytical profession.

Life Path Number 8

You are an ambitious hardworking, practical, and a down to earth leader, who is a good judge of character and has high ideals and expectations. You display outstanding entrepreneurial skills and can generate significant wealth and power. However, for you to be successful, you need to live with the utmost integrity, helping and serving others.

You would excel at running your own business or be a team leader, manager, or business advisor.

Life Path Number 9

You are a compassionate and caring humanitarian, and it is important for you to make the world a better place through teaching and sharing your vast knowledge. However, before you can achieve this, you need to learn not to judge others and to accept not only their faults and imperfections but your own too.

You may be drawn to humanitarian, charity work, teaching or public services, where you feel you can make a difference.

Life Path Number 11

You have a natural ability to inspire and to teach others. You are here to make a difference and to work for the greater good. You need to ensure that you do not give too much of yourself to others and learn to say no.

Similar to life path 2, you would flourish in anything caring or in a supporting role such as counsellor, psychologist, teacher or being a motivational speaker.

Life Path Number 22

You are here as the master builder and have great vision. You create and build projects seeing them through to completion and are here to create something that can help and benefit others. It is important that you can remain focused and be disciplined so that you can create, build, and fulfil your dreams.

You would be a good architect, scientist, or engineer. Similar to life path 4, you would also make a good personal assistant, manager, or business owner.

Life Path Number 33

You are helpful, sensitive, and understanding and are here to support and to care for others. Number 33's work well with children and would make wonderful parents. Similar to life path number 6 you need to find a balance between helping and not interfering.

You would make a good motivational speaker, healer, teacher, doctor, counsellor, or therapist.

THE DESTINY NUMBERS

Also known as your expression number, your destiny number indicates your mission and purpose in life.

Destiny Number 1

You are destined to be an independent leader. You are a great self-starter and have the confidence and courage to make things happen with a high chance of success. You do not like routine and prefer to be busy and to look at the bigger picture, allowing others to worry about the finer details.

Destiny Number 2

Your destiny is to help and support others through your capacity to be a natural peacemaker and mediator. You work well with people and shy away from personal recognition. You will grow through gaining a better understanding of the people around you.

Destiny Number 3

You are destined to inspire motivate and bring happiness to others through your creative and artistic capabilities. You are warm, friendly, and sociable and you strive to be a good friend to others.

Destiny Number 4

You are destined to find order and stability within your workplace and family preferring to be well organised and focusing on attention to detail. Creating stability with a secure life is most important to you.

Destiny Number 5

You are destined to be a free spirit enjoying new experiences and living life to the full. It is important that you share and teach your experiences with others promoting change and new ideas. You are not a completer finisher and can sometimes have a scatter gun approach to life.

Destiny Number 6

You are destined to love and support others through your kind, caring and sympathetic nature. You are open and honest and feel responsible to help and to heal those around you in whatever way you can.

Destiny Number 7

You enjoy working alone and can study complex subjects, seeking to become a specialist in your field by gaining knowledge and a deeper understanding to the meaning of life. You prefer your own company and can be antisocial, inflexible, and intolerant of others.

Destiny Number 8

You seek to achieve power and success through managing your own business or helping others who do not have your strong leadership skills to success. You are extremely capable and confident and can be impatient with others. It is important that you are considerate to others and that you use your talents wisely.

Destiny Number 9

You seek to make the world a better place by learning to be non-judgemental and helping others with compassion love and kindness. Friendships and supporting and inspiring others are important to you.

Destiny Number 11

You seek to teach and inspire others to reach their full potential by promoting peace and harmony and gaining their own spiritual awareness. You can sometimes be impractical and can get frustrated when others do not see the bigger picture.

Destiny Number 22

You seek to help others with your hard working, practical and logical approach. You can fulfil your ambitions and dreams, turning them into reality. It is important that you remain focused and do not become distracted with limiting beliefs of your capabilities.

Destiny Number 33

You are here to serve and to help others. You are deeply compassionate, sacrificing your own needs to bring peace, love joy and harmony to the world.

THE SOUL NUMBERS

Also known as your heart's desire, the soul number indicates the desires that influence your life.

Soul Number 1

Ambitious and seeking recognition for your achievements is what makes you content. You are a determined individual who likes to work independently from others.

Soul Number 2

Love, friendship, peace, and harmony are most important to you. Ensuring that your friends, work colleagues and the environment around you is harmonious and full of love is your heart's desire.

Soul Number 3

Expressing your creativity through laughter, the arts and having fun and good conversation is important to you and makes you feel happy and content. You need to be joyful and happy and believe that you must live life to the full.

Soul Number 4

Being secure financially and professionally, and having a stable life is important to you. You are hardworking, focused, and conscientious and you do not like uncertainty and sudden change. You are content working towards routine and order.

Soul Number 5

You live for freedom and adventure and will be inspired and exited by learning new things, travel, new experiences and meeting new people. Living for today is important to you.

Soul Number 6

You will feel complete every time you offer love, support, and affection to your family and those around you. Living in harmony, offering stability, and feeling needed will bring you happiness.

Soul Number 7

You can feel awkward and shy around people and you are happiest when alone with your thoughts spending your time seeking wisdom.

Soul Number 8

Success and power in your personal life and your work are what drives you. You are at your best when leading others to success and you thrive on responsibility and challenges.

Soul Number 9

Helping others and bringing peace love and harmony and working for the greater good is important to you.

Soul Number 11

Helping to guide others to improve and to reach their full potential by sharing your ideas and promoting peace and harmony to all is important to you.

Soul Number 22

Feeling that you have contributed and made a difference through your vision and hard work that benefits others is important to you.

Soul Number 33

It is important to make the world a better place through serving those in need and teaching love and happiness.

PERSONALITY NUMBERS

Your personality number represents the side of yourself that you are willing to let others see.

Personality Number 1

You will be seen by others as the capable go to person in charge who is confident and happy to lead and to take control. You can be seen to be aggressive and you like to do things your way.

Personality Number 2

You are warm, kind-hearted, friendly, and approachable. You love to socialise and enjoy organising events and gatherings. You have a caring nature and have a genuine desire to help and to bring out the best in everyone.

Personality Number 3

You are friendly and charismatic and want to be popular and the centre of attention. You are great to have at a party and people will be drawn to you and feel uplifted by your charm and wit.

Personality Number 4

You want to be relied upon by others for your expertise hard work and professionalism and it is important for you to be looked upon as trustworthy, responsible, and honest.

Personality Number 5

You are a charming confident individual who can be very persuasive. People will be drawn to you as you have the capability to show an interest and to talk to everyone. You can become easily distracted and you need to work at keeping focused.

Personality Number 6

You are wise and caring and someone that will offer a shoulder to cry on. Because you take your responsibilities seriously, you can take on too much as you find it hard to say no. You can tend to get too involved in other people's problems and be too opinionated.

Personality Number 7

You are a loner, preferring your own company whilst looking for the answers to life mysteries. People will look to you for your knowledge and wisdom, but you can be difficult to befriend due to your lack of trust in others.

Personality Number 8

You are seen by others to be a natural confident, strong leader who effortlessly takes control. Your image and status are important to you as is your material wealth.

Personality Number 9

You are seen by others to be caring, compassionate and supportive of others. You can sometimes be too sensitive, so it is important that you accept others without judgement, or you could be viewed as intolerant and volatile.

Personality Number 11

You are an outgoing, charismatic visionary who feels that there is more to life. People will be drawn to your enthusiasm and inspiration.

Personality Number 22

You are a hard-working, committed visionary who wants to turn your dreams into a reality. Others will seek your help and look to you for advice and guidance.

Personality Number 33

You are compassionate and kind and put the good of others before yourself, working towards their happiness and well-being.

THE MATURITY NUMBERS

Referring to the later part of your life. Your maturity number shows your future potential and your ultimate goal.

Maturity Number 1

As you mature you will find the courage to achieve your goals and to move towards having more freedom and being more confident and independent. You will focus on helping others with kindness and compassion.

Maturity Number 2

As you mature you will become more sensitive and have a better understanding of those around you. You are moving closer to finding peace and harmony and overcoming conflicts in others.

Maturity Number 3

As you mature you will become even more sociable with the ability to inspire uplift and bring joy to others through your creative and communicative abilities.

Maturity Number 4

You are moving towards a time of success and accomplishment bringing stability and order at work and within your family. You are becoming more focused with your achievements and goals.

Maturity Number 5

You are moving towards more travel and freedom and will become more adventurous. You will get bored more easily as there are so many new places to see and people to meet.

Maturity Number 6

You are working towards becoming more involved, offering more love, support, protection and advice to your friends and family.

Maturity Number 7

You are moving towards being able to increase your knowledge and wisdom, spending more time in thought, meditation, and contemplation.

Maturity Number 8

As you mature you will become more focused on your career and material success. It is important for you to feel needed by others and to raise your status in the workplace.

Maturity Number 9

As you mature you will be working towards helping others who are less fortunate, and you may also grow to appreciate and to enjoy the arts.

Maturity Number 11

You are moving towards a deeper intuitive nature, helping, and inspiring others to reach their full potential.

Maturity Number 22

You will be moving towards advising, supporting, and teaching others within your community. Working as a leader or project manager supporting others to reach their potential is a possibility.

Maturity Number 33

You are raising your intuition and working towards bringing love and happiness in the world through caring and offering your love and kindness to others.

THE BIRTH DAY NUMBERS

Your birth day number will reveal talents that can help you whilst on your life path.

Birth Day Number 1

You are born to lead and have a strong and dynamic personality. You often find yourself being the centre of attention, however you can be sensitive and hide your feelings. You need to work at not being too impatient and intolerant of others.

Birth Day Number 2

You are born to work in harmony in a team environment and like to bring out the best in others. You are warm hearted and can make friends easily. Relationships are particularly important to you however you do not seek the limelight and are far happier working behind the scenes.

Birth Day Number 3

You are outgoing and a great communicator with a fantastic sense of humour, however you do have a sensitive side and will be very aware of other people's feelings.

Birth Day Number 4

You like to be in control and can be inflexible and have a stubborn streak. Although you find it hard to show your feelings you are a loyal partner and friend and will always do the right thing. Your serious hardworking approach to life will ensure your success.

Birth Day Number 5

You like change and are capable of being versatile and learning new things. You have a quick and analytical mind, enjoy new experiences and can be very adaptable. You can become restless and impatient. It is important to accept responsibility and to seek balance in your life.

Birth Day Number 6

You are loving, and kind and with your sympathetic nature, you can counsel, heal, and support those around you.

Birth Day Number 7

You are highly intuitive and have a deeper understanding and awareness than the other numbers. You are sensitive and do not like to be told what to do, preferring to spend time alone enjoying nature and the outdoors where you can meditate and explore not only complex subjects, such as science and physics but also the meaning of life.

Birth Day Number 8

You are extremely business minded and can successfully organise and manage people. It is important that you do not spend all your time focusing on wealth and power but use your influence to spend some time on worthwhile causes.

Birth Day Number 9

You are generous with your time and have an understanding towards the needs of others and their feelings. You are idealistic and sensitive which means that you can find yourself in challenging situations, finding it hard to forgive and to let go of other people's failings.

Birth Day Number 11

You can be sensitive and sometimes confuse feelings and emotions of others as your own. You can inspire and help others, but it is important that you shield yourself from their emotions and feelings.

Birth Day Number 22

You are logical, organised, and capable of bringing projects and plans to fruition. It is important that you overcome the sensitivity of the double 2s in your chart and focus on working for the benefit of others.

CONNECTING YOUR NUMBERS

Once you have calculated your core numbers you need to find a way of combining and making a connection between them. To help with this process you need to focus on the base meanings of your numbers.

It is important to remember that there are good qualities and not so good qualities in the numbers, and it is therefore up to you to identify which is relevant to you personally. If you find that you have 2 or more numbers that are the same within your chart it can sometimes mean that you have an important challenge held within the number to overcome.

Making a connection will be based on your own interpretation and there is no right or wrong way to do this. Once you have a better understanding of numerology you will be able to use your intuition to interpret the connections between them.

Go back to the chart on page 33 to use as an aid to help you with this.

Now that you have been introduced to your core numbers you will be able to have a far better understanding of where you are heading with your life, helping you to identify your strengths and weakness, and revealing the true you. You will also be clearer on what motivates and drives you and understand why you react to situations around you in a certain way. This understanding will enable you to move forward and be the best that you can be.

This is only the beginning and just a basic overview however there are so many more calculations that you can do.

I urge you to start to use numerology to compliment your life. Remember that numbers are all around you and once you take notice of them, they can help to guide you through difficult or important stages of your life such as when to change careers, move home or get married.

I was surprised when I recently identified that the house number at my old house matched my life path number which is 5. Number 5's walk the path of freedom and exploration and want to live life to the full. It is also important that 5's are free to explore and to experience everything that life has to offer and that they feel challenged and fulfilled in all that they do.

I moved into this house as my second marriage was failing and remained there with my son after we divorced. It was during this time there that I was able to progress at work and achieve 2 promotions. The promotions enabled me to be more flexible with my hours and with a higher salary helped me with my sons schooling. I was also able to renovate my home from top to bottom and I also invested in a small studio flat that I renovated which was a dream of mine and was extremely rewarding. However, after 28 years of working for a large life and medical insurance company I was made redundant. I enjoyed working there as it gave me the variety of work that number 5's crave, and the flexibility and the financial security that I needed being a single parent, but I always felt that I wanted to be free and to be my own boss. I could have played it safe and applied for other roles within the company but redundancy gave me the opportunity that I had been longing for and so I took a big leap of faith and became self-employed. I had obtained considerable medical knowledge in my previous roles, so I decided to re-train as a Foot Health Professional and while my son was studying for his GCSE exams, I was keeping him company by studying Foot Health. After I qualified, I started up my own Foot Health practice, initially converting my lounge to a treatment room with all the equipment that was required to run a professional practice. When I became more successful with over 250 patients visiting me regularly, I re-configured the house so that I had a separate treatment room with a waiting room accessed from the side of the house. It was one of the most rewarding and empowering things that I have ever done, and surprisingly my house number also complimented my soul number which is also number 5!

This was the catalyst that I needed and has opened the door to not only treating and helping people with a vast array of foot complaints but also listening to their problems and realising that my role is far from just treating their feet! This has led on to further training to study as a mindfulness and meditation coach and a numerologist. I feel that I am now on the right path and I would encourage anyone who may be dissatisfied with their life to spend some time understanding themselves and what is important to them either through numerology or meditation and mindfulness and to make the change. Easy for a number 5 to say!

Now that you have been introduced to numerology, why not try to calculate your friends and family's numbers? You will then have a better understanding of who they are, their life challenges and what motivates them. You will be amazed at what they will reveal to you!

Printed in Great Britain
by Amazon